se for Sugar Water

"*In the highly charged and deeply felt world of Brad Beau Cohen's poetry, eroticism is both complex and enigmatic as 'denim-clad deities' cruise the beach at night and breath becomes 'a sodium spark on skin'. These poems are bold, off-kilter and surreal examinations of queer life and desire. Though there are wounds here, as a poem becomes a cell, 'storm-wrung' or 'drawn with blood', the work ultimately proclaims survival.*"

– Richard Scott, author of Soho (Faber)

"*These are poems to float on, to drown in. Intimate and unshrinking, Sugar Water takes its themes from the body, queerness, memory and pain. Cohen's work has a dark, glittering eroticism; alert to form and with a thirst for the image. To read Sugar Water is to savour the spirit of what is fresh in current poetry.*"

-Ella Duffy, author of Rootstalk (Hazel Press) and New Hunger (Smith | Doorstop)

SUGAR WATER

Brad Beau Cohen

Peter — my wonderful queer-po
Siblings! Thank you for never-
ending support & love.
    I hope you enjoy the
        final swell.
    Big love.

        S. Cen

SOHO CITY BOOKS

PUBLISHED BY SOHO CITY BOOKS 2022

2 4 6 8 10 9 7 5 3

First published in 2022 by
SOHO CITY BOOKS

www.sohocitybooks.com

ISBN 978 1 3999 1865 7 (Paperback edition)

Typeset in Book Antiqua by SOHO CITY BOOKS

Cover design by Brad Beau Cohen

for Kelly

and all other siblings-in-survival

SUGAR WATER

Contents

Hungry Him

He disturbs the bed
super-imposing crumpled sheets
like a mistake left

on a page, proof
of impatience
with a hunger for lead

or an artist's tongue
to draw a line, on hips
virile brackets to exist

within he'll pour himself
to the brim, then paint heavenly
frescos on your heavy eyelids

that tell lies so beguiling
like a dead man's iris
blooming a moon

that rises like bone
to break the skin
of oblivious night

and when you shout in thanks
like a war-time surrender
he'll fill you up to drown you out

A Mother Introduces the Storm

Rain comes
eliminating the sky
with glass shards that fall
to make heads bow

my clothes
now cold parentheses
expose the limits of my skin

wind-whipped waves
      double the rain
            bay flailing
                  like a dying eel

and I brought us here
to the shoreline
that's trying to recruit my son
as silt tugs at his toes
while he giggles

he knows how electricity
smells in the air
and it's my fault
his eyes will remember
big cinema
his skin - salt

his cells
the element

a rock pool grows
        bleeding navy inheritance
                        into the next

at the inaugural crack
he raises bloated fists
little tongue hanging
like a petal
waiting to taste
the first drop of the storm

The Tower

I

Mum stands behind the bar

o-faced pupils line the sticky varnished wood
learning how to drown sorrows from the best

she leaves
casting her classroom motherless

she answers the landline
and entertains a man with a grudge

another class she could teach so well

II

if cups are the suit of emotion
this public house must be
a library of private pain, stacked
with limescale-white covers, flaps
of skin that flutter back

                              epiphanous

III

a pair of halogen lights glare
through the face of us, uncurtained
eyes double-glazed
while cement fists hold my ankles
trembling but set
like my grandfather's

IV

s t e e l m e e t s s t e e l *bone*   *l*   *i*
                            flash t h e *n* *f*   *t*
                                      a   *l*   *e*
                                            n

V

a bullet-silver car sits livid
in the ventricle of the lounge bar
hollow tip ticking like an electrified needle
and dust injected into the air between
like some primal hormone

VI

war planet bricks spill
from the bay window
onto the pavement and I
taste the minerals I
touch my cupid's bow
and prescribed
on my fingertips
is our shared wound

Water & Stone

The tide is trying to swallow the perimeter of the bathing pool. A sandstone crescent with rusted handrails three feet high reminds me of Roman ruins and how I imagine my mum's cell to look. Prison's taken the hypolimnion current from her words and she writes to me every week. I haven't replied, afraid that I'll fail again at playing my role as life-raft. Denial isn't something I've ever been good at - ocean eyes betray my shallows. A final swell erases the blueprint of the bathing pool, leaving only the bars.

Haloed feet bring me to the hem, in the wind I unravel. One thread to hold me here, one for each of my mothers and one to keep the poem running. Cobbles cast themselves at my feet, asking me to dance. A wave retreats, pulling golden ribbons across my toes. The water in me pinches for permission, patient until gunshot lightning sends teardrops ploughing across the pink fields of my cheeks. They leap to return home and my biology can't help it. Salt sings with it. A want to fall back into the deepest cup. That blue basin spilling over year by year.

Would I tell her the sea is still trying to adopt me? The territories of motherhood are cruel, as she knows. A boulder-roll of thunder sends a flock of seagulls screeching from the beach. And the waves keep coming, with more pebbles that hop water-brained at my ankles. A choreography depicting the softening of stone. Small traumas begging. Begging for me to play.

Deep End

Concern yourself with where to simmer -
in broken water is where you choose

bladderwrack skin nap shiver
of fishbones choke the pipes

driftwood candles a blown out wish
for deep end reek and acoustics

that ring out to explain away
the storm-wrung bath detritus

La Lune

In me you saw a madness
velvet and indigo I slipped
sebum-slick into our night sky
wandering through car parks on piers
and forest trails
they say my face betrays
my past, and you
because somehow I still blush
on cue
what a trick
a cruel young trick
I must be living
too close to the sea
learning with her other children
to make lies sing
you see -
to survive him, I pretended
to be older, to survive for you
I pretend to be youthful
the full truth is a
moonstone
somewhere between
phases and gradients of grey
but divining it doesn't help us now -
me, covered in piss from

dreaming of a past I deny
is only three months away from me
you, promising a kiss
can help a rusting ship to float
despite your organs
sinking like a foghorn
swim to shore
your pedigree is begging you
and now is not our time
we say in our final act
of unison, voices eclipsed
then
pleading dumb at my bleeding moons
you bend as if over a corpse
ear to heart
and hear nothing but the ocean

a bird, a boyfriend

in featherless flight
you left

a brood of windows
blind to beg

for faces
as lubricious surfaces do

                    in glassy grief
          they squeeze my room

              made brick balloon
           and without a bribe

                 I feel a breach
             might come soon

Arrested for Buggery, GY1 2008

Brick, sandstone, breeze block
or other
    I once spent an hour painting nicotine on the walls
                      of a cell
in the tradition of my gorgeous rainbow ancestors
but this
                inheritance was given by a rapist
                      an arrest
for buggery with free cigarettes
for survival
                while the policeman invoked
                      his sigils
formality, protocol, procedure
or other
            while the policewoman invoked her own
                      sorry silence
despite hearing five hours of young agony
stop short
    the interview after disclosure of the victim's crime
                    written neon red
a flashing sign you can't recant so
tell them
    about the vacant room with yellowing wallpaper
                    on brick
or breeze block, or other, one of the three
long years

it took to calcify so they can float you for a fortnight
to then be told
no charges will be brought, you waited too long
or other

How You Are Here

Night bucked
and sent you skimming
across a body of bricks

so you take time to tally
the rare things
that open for you
mango skin   zip flies

and the glossy fold
of a faux-leather wallet
dropped to the asphalt

this spine
is the only clean line
more perfect than cocaine
and not yet piss-wet
but now winks
the gold threat of dawn

When Skin Won't Sleep

He sleeps   with winter windows   open
                                                hoping

the itch   will contain itself   like cold

water   that can't lift   can't creep
      from

between threads.
                  Still   he unravels himself

                                                nightly
with fingernails to pick
                  skipped stitches
                              and pulls
red ribbon
            rivers from the dermis.

Pale bedsheets are the enemy
                              canvas of
sleepless past

predators
            terracotta as cave walls
                                          drawn
with blood

in an artist's trance   fevered half-sleep

brings sweat
      with salt to prickle
             skin, stripped

pyjamas chase his waist
       like seaweed

in the bed turning
       rock pool.

The ceiling foams

      livid white   and slaps him

with a wave

      each morning   he wakes

to drown

      another night.

At the Bathing Pools

Even as a child I knew
that spilt drinks are followed by swift exits
so as I saw the rose lemonade
fizz across the sky, I wasn't surprised

by my grandmother's hurried hands
drawing me up as I dripped with brine
beads of wetness that darkened the tarmac
like a broken necklace left behind

through the car window
I saw families pluck themselves
from the beach, flick towels
to loosen sand, unmute flags
that waved proud and brief
before retreat

men emerged
as we drove by
uncovered by headlights
peeking through bushes
with their amber eyes
like matchsticks striking
for a desperate moment

I learned at sixteen
why they haunt the man-made bay

and straddle the rock-sharp tip
of the moon's silver tongue
as it rests breathless
on the water

there
where each minute chases morning
your new god stands behind you
lends a master hand
only taking small bribes of salt
licked from the trough of your back
spine buried under the flesh
of a jasmine petal

then
you fade to black
and pearls roll back
into the navy boil of night
but when swimmers
reclaim the waters
these denim-clad deities
will have no new daughters

Pink Friction

Seed
between beak
my nipple punctuates
its surrender
to your teeth

masc dampened
by the act
doped
as a straight boy
after his first
finger

your lawless tongue
non-Newtonian
flicks a lick
like a striking match
along a line
of pink friction

then breath
a
        sodium
                    spark
        on   skin
                    made   wet

Shadow Play

Our shadows merge
birthed from eggshell

like strange silent birds
that flap with us

but exaggerate curves
& mock proportions

the physics of them
bent

by a meaning
we should interpret

this Rorschach flock
while our moment's

un
murdered

Playground

You come round to play
the game that makes us
childish architects at night
we stack our colourful promises
high as building blocks
to fall as we dance around
primary plastic eggshells
painful as bricks
we stick
to the subject of our sex
while nimble fingers
paint practiced shapes
thumbed circumferences
& circles like stick man heads
around heads & nipples
& crêpe paper holes
as delicate as our roles
for one word out of line
could split these territories
a story of two new enemies
waging war
on their own playground

A new breed of mantis cuts the air

                   with a reach
                       that could
bloom spines   to forget legs
            or left forget right
                tongue forget tongue
his screen's unlocked
         head bowed in private prayer
                  dons a mask of
orange neon
        severe as the sunset
              that slices the bedroom

in a clash
      two shades of epoch
            skins rejecting their stitches

our sewn seconds now phantom-felt
                                 fade
to before
          when we were one
                language of limbs
                     conjoined as
creature
       cut in two by his device
                   and I'm still glazed
                     with his fluids

Shy Pry Lover

In afterglow
on prayer elbows
he looks for a circle
above my head
      but finds vultures instead

with a slow toke
his pass lingers
as if it's made dangerous
between my fingers
      smoke curling with his suspicion

smack-dragged lips
over teeth
sound a nervous smile
I taste the question
      he lets the air eat

then
a bluff kiss at the door
when he forgets politeness
tilts his head
      in once-and-for-all

Sugar Water

Boys never stay
to taste the seasoned skin
it's a treasure to be saved
for when wicks are waxless
& smoke floats tidal

let the room of ghosts watch
your taking of stock
tally with the tongue
whispered *fucks* wrapped
around knuckles

with curl ribbons of left breath
la petite mort &
borrowed cologne
wilting on your lips
like a stone-side bouquet

find the jewel in your belly button
a molten mother-of-pearl
then taste that sugar water
biology of both
& anoint your cupid's bow

map uncharted hip riches
edgings of seminal lace

veins of gold on your bruised ass
& when your smile bankrupts the moon
know you gave yourself these gifts

Immortal Metal

after *Lady Lazarus*

This is number four
each time there's a rush of air
with a glint

quick squint
& the shock of hearing
as it sings against skin

the younger silver crescent
swiped down from stars to mark me
is a chipped immortal metal

a smile with missing teeth
typecast as horror movie villain
you could say he has a call

donning his stage-black costume
face veiled with thin recognition
the flavour of minor funeral celebrity

then realisation blooms
like the nightly applause
of lotus petals

their screaming rebirth
a performance that promises
bouquets

white roses
smacking wood
in honour of the star

on a farewell tour
before the curtains close
like palm on throat

now you see
I am the thing
that blunts the Reaper's blade

Church

Wall to mantel the choirs of statues blaze, but no virgin's glare could annul our sermon. Blow argent smoke from your mouth, a pink and porcelain censer. Grey curls bloom in amber light from the streetlamp, ghost lilies in our urban Eden. A drop gives in and plays lead on the glass stained by our breath.

Newborn, my arms hang from your shoulders, ankles crossed with yours. Your chin prickles my forehead. We are a carnal crucifix. Blood-rust rings from my glass brand a triquetra on your stomach: still tense. Five disciples stroke my scalp, run through the sweat-knot scourge. My knees weep on the ivory-white sheet from my last pillow-less confession.

Silent in your possession, an echoing hymn of exhalation. Your communion is a spatter on the mattress, already soaked in. Cool constellations on my calf. Here in our sanctuary, there's a murmuring crusade, their huffing organs a dirge to grind to. A few muted thuds from upstairs. Our voyeur above enjoyed the show.

NEXT

Rose Jam

With knees foam-sheathed
she pins the brown soil
unwilling body of earth
until sundown it's hers
the grandmother, mother, widow
whisperer to the world
beneath her, families
of spiders scurry and ants
dance for their priestess
as she snips carmine planets
from their sky that hit the ground
exploded
petals crushed between
her sandalled toes
rose jam boiling in the air
she continues her ruthless work
for thankless generations

Acknowledgements

Many thanks go to the publications that first published the pieces in *Sugar Water,* including Fourteen Poems, Fincham Press, Versification Zine. Huge appreciation to my dearest friend and patron, R. White, my sister Kelly, Jess, Smomo, Cecil and the Lamé Foil group for your never-ending support and reading the seeds of these poems. Huge gratitude to Sian Williams (film), Maurizio Bongiovanni (painting), Jessica Rae Lewis (illustration) and Rosie Taylor (music) for bringing these poems to life through your art. Thank you Richard Scott, Ben from Fourteen Poems, Jonathan Kemp and Ella Duffy for your generous and kind words of endorsement.

Immortal Metal is inspired by Sylvia Plath's *Lady Lazarus* (Ariel, Faber and Faber, 1965).

Author biography

Brad Beau Cohen's (he/him/they/them) poetry has been published worldwide by Fourteen Poems, Elska Magazine, American literary journal Versification Zine, anthologised twice by Fincham Press, and exhibited in The Hilbert Raum and SomosArt House. Some of his poems have been adapted into film by Sian Williams and were catalogued by the BFI, screened at FRINGE queer film festival, Leeds Queer Film Festival, FEST and shortlisted for the ShanghaiPRIDE Film Festival. Cohen is a queer writer from Guernsey based in London. This is Cohen's debut poetry pamphlet. His social handles on Instagram and Twitter are @bradbeaucohen

Lightning Source UK Ltd.
Milton Keynes UK
UKHW042127230222
399150UK00001B/233

9 781399 918657